W9-CBN-608

WITHDRAWN

The Exclusions of a Rhyme

Poems and Epigrams

The Exclusions of a Rhyme

Poems and Epigrams

BY J. V. CUNNINGHAM

Alan Swallow

DENVER

TO MY WIFE

And does the heart grow old? You know
In the indiscriminate green
Of summer or in earliest snow
A landscape is another scene,

Inchoate and anonymous,
And every rock and bush and drift
As our affections alter us
Will alter with the season's shift.

So love by love we come at last,
As through the exclusions of a rhyme,
Or the exactions of a past,
To the simplicity of time,

The antiquity of grace, where yet
We live in terror and delight
With love as quiet as regret
And love like anger in the night.

Certain of the poems in this collection were first published in the author's *The Helmsman* (San Francisco, 1942), *The Judge Is Fury* (New York, 1947), *Doctor Drink* (Cummington, Mass., 1950), *The Quest of the Opal* (Denver, 1950), The Augustan Reprint Society pamphlet, number 24 (Los Angeles, 1950), and in the following magazines and anthologies: *Commonweal, Hound and Horn, New York Times, The Magazine, Modern Verse, Trial Balances* (New York, 1936), *Twelve Poets of the Pacific* (Norfolk, Conn., 1937), *New Mexico Quarterly Review, Arizona Quarterly, Poetry, Philological Quarterly, New Poems by American Poets* (New York, 1953), *Poems in Folio* (San Francisco, 1957), and *Partisan Review.*

Contents

The Helmsman

The Judge Is Fury

Doctor Drink

Trivial, Vulgar, and Exalted

Translations from the Latin

The Exclusions of a Rhyme

Poems and Epigrams

The Helmsman

1942

Of thirty years ten years I gave to rhyme
That this time should not pass: so passes time.

Poets survive in fame.
But how can substance trade
The body for a name
Wherewith no soul's arrayed?

No form inspires the clay
Now breathless of what was
Save the imputed sway
Of some Pythagoras,

Some man so deftly mad
His metamorphosed shade,
Leaving the flesh it had,
Breathes on the words they made.

THE WANDERING SCHOLAR'S PRAYER
TO ST. CATHERINE OF EGYPT

Past ruined cities down the grass,
Past wayside smokers in the shade,
Clicking their heels the fruit cars pass
Old stations where the night is stayed.

Curved on the racking wheel's retreat,
Sweet Catherine, rise from time to come!
Number in pain the fruit car fleet,
And throw confusion in the sum!

The vagrants smoke in solitude,
Sick of the spittle without cough.
Not unabsolved do they grow rude,
Dying with Swift in idiot froth.

From revery, sweet saint, forfend
These ravelled faces of the park!
When questing cars at twilight's end
Cozen the eyes with chilling dark,

Save them from memory of the light,
The circuit of the orient sun
Wheeling loud silence through the night
Like headlamps where the twin rails run.

THE DOG-DAYS

hic in reducta valle Caniculae
vitabis aestus . . .

The morning changes in the sun
As though the hush were insecure,
And love, so perilously begun,
Could never in the noon endure,

The noon of unachieved intent,
Grown hazy with unshadowed light,
Where changing is subservient
To hope no longer, nor delight.

Nothing alive will stir for hours,
Dispassion will leave love unsaid,
While through the window masked with flowers
A lone wasp staggers from the dead.

Watch now, bereft of coming days,
The wasp in the darkened chamber fly,
Whirring ever in an airy maze,
Lost in the light he entered by.

ELEGY FOR A CRICKET

at vobis male sit, malae tenebrae
Orci, quae omnia bella devoratis!

Fifteen nights I have lain awake and called you
But you walk ever on and give no answer:
Therefore, damned by my sole, go down to hellfire.
Spirit luminous and footstep uncertain,
You will pace off forever the halls of great Dis.
You there, caught in the whirling throng of lovers,
If you find in that fire her whom I loved once,
Say to her that I gave you few but true words.
Say to her that your dream as her dream held me,
Alone, waking, until your friend, the cock, slept.
Say to her, if she ask what shoe you wear now,
That I gave you my last, I have none other.

This dry and lusty wind has stirred all night
The tossing forest of one sleepless tree,
And I in waking vision walked with her
Whose hair hums to the motion of the forest
And in the orbit of whose eyelids' fall
The clouds drift slowly from the starry wharves.
I knew her body well but could not speak,
For comprehension is a kind of silence,
The last harmonic of all sound. Europa,
Iö, and Danäe: their names are love
Incarnate in the chronicles of love.
I trace their sad initials which thy bark,
Gaunt tree, may line with age but not efface,
And carve her name with mine there. The tree is gnarled
And puckered as a child that looks away
And fumbles at the breast—prodigious infant
Still sucking at the haggard teats of time!
Radical change, the root of human woe!

All choice is error, the tragical mistake,
And you are mine because I name you mine.
Kiss, then, in pledge of the imponderables
That tilt the balance of eternity
A leaf's weight up and down. Though we must part
While each dawn darkens on the fortunate wheel,
The moon will not soften our names cut here
Till every sheltering bird has fled the nest.

They know the wind brings rain, and rain and wind
Will smooth the outlines of our lettering
To the simplicity of epitaph.

OBSEQUIES FOR A POETESS

Kathleen Tankersley Young, 1933

The candles gutter in her quiet room,
And retrospect, returning through the sad
Degrees of dusk that had o'ershadowed pain,
Finds her Lethean source, the unmemoried stream
Of cold sensation. There, vain Sibylls clothed
In solemn ash, their hair dishevelled, weep
The close of centuries where time like stanzas
Stands in division, disposed, and none
Dare chant antiphonal to that strain. Pale Aubrey
Finds there his faint and final rest; there Dowson
Pillows his fond head on each breast. For them
And their compeers, our blind and exiled ghosts
Which nightly gull us with oblivion,
Weave we this garland of deciduous bloom
With subtle thorn. Their verse, sepulchral, breathes
A careless scent of flowers in late July,
Too brief for pleasure, though its pleasure lie
In skilled inconscience of its brevity.

Over the heady wine,
Well-watered with good sense,
Come, sing the simple line
And charm confusion hence.

The fathers on the shelves
Surely approve our toasts,
Surely are here themselves,
Warm, amiable ghosts,

Glad to escape the new
Regenerate elect
Who take the social view
And zealously reject

The classic indignation,
The sullen clarity
Of passions in their station,
Moved by propriety.

Men give their hearts away;
Whether for good or ill
    They cannot say
Who shape the object in their will.

The will in pure delight
Conceives itself. I praise
    Far lamps at night,
Cold landmarks for reflection's gaze.

Distant they still remain,
Oh, unassailed, apart!
    May time attain
The promise ere death seals the heart!

Keep the quick eyes hid in your mind!
Unleash them when the game is spied!
Free-reined fancy will but make blind
Your carnal soul, flesh glorified.

But firm fancy, untimely stayed,
Fixed on the one shape, still rehearsed,
Becomes the idol that it made,
Possessed by pure matter, accursed.

The hot flesh and passionless mind
In fancy's house must still abide,
Each share the work, its share defined
By caution under custom's guide.

THE HELMSMAN: AN ODE

The voyage of the soul is simply
   Through age to wisdom;
      But wisdom, if it comes,
Comes like the ripening gleam of wheat,

Nourished by comfort, care, rain, sunlight,
   And briefly shining
      On windy and hot days,
Flashing like snakes underneath the haze.

But this, a memory of childhood,
   Of loves forgotten,
      And they who gave are still,
Gone now, irrevocable, undone.

O Penury, steadied to thy will,
   I tread my own path,
      Though Self-Respect, discreet,
Plucks at my arm as I pass down street:—

Querulous and pert! They tell in story
   That for proud Ajax,
      Vaingloriously self-slain,
Teucer set forth from his friends and kin;

He on the western shore of parting
   Paused to address them:
      "Comrades who have with me
Countless misfortunes endured, O mine!

Brave friends, banish tonight dark sorrow!
    Set the white tables
        With garlands, lamps, with wine!
    Drink! and, tomorrow, untravelled seas!"

So sailed guileful Odysseus, so sailed
    Pious Aeneas,
        And cloudless skies brought sleep,
    Stilling th' unmasterable, surging deep—

The helmsman stilled, his sea-craft guiding.
    O too confiding
        In star and wind and wave,
    Naked thou liest in an unknown grave!

Fickle mankind!
When force and change
Wildly derange
The casual mind
   On chance begotten,

Trust in the Lord,
For that is best.
As for the rest,
Though not ignored
   And not forgotten,

The heart not whole
Nor quite at ease,
Here finds some peace,
Some wealth of soul—
   Albeit ill-gotten.

Then leave old regret,
Ancestral remorse,
Which, though you forget,
Unseen keep their course;

Shaping what each says,
Weathered in his style,
They in his fond ways
Live on for a while.

But leave them at last
To find their own home.
Inured to the past,
Be what you become:

Nor ungrudgingly
Your young hours dispense,
Nor live curiously,
Cheating providence.

Most beautiful, most dear!
When I would use Thy light,
Beloved, omniscient Seer,
Thou didst abuse my sight:

Thou didst pervade my being
Like marsh air steeped in brine;
Thou didst invade my seeing
Till all I saw was Thine.

Today, from my own fence
I saw the grass fires rise,
And saw Thine old incense
Borne up in frosty sighs!

Most terrible, most rude!
I will not shed a tear
For lost beatitude,
But I still fear Thy fear.

SUMMER IDYLL

There is a kind of privacy
Immobile as the windless wheat
Within whose dusty seignory
We ripen with maturing heat—

Dreamless repose, unvisioned rest,
Gold harvest that we will not reap,
Perfect the sleeper on your breast!
And if he wake not? He will sleep.

CHOICE

Allegiance is assigned
Forever when the mind
Chooses and stamps the will.
Thus, I must love you still
Through good and ill.

But though we cannot part
We may retract the heart
And build such privacies
As self-regard agrees
Conduce to ease.

So manners will repair
The ravage of despair
Which generous love invites,
Preferring quiet nights
To vain delights.

FOR MY CONTEMPORARIES

How time reverses
The proud in heart!
I now make verses
Who aimed at art.

But I sleep well.
Ambitious boys
Whose big lines swell
With spiritual noise,

Despise me not!
And be not queasy
To praise somewhat:
Verse is not easy.

But rage who will.
Time that procured me
Good sense and skill
Of madness cured me.

1. *An Epitaph for Anyone*

An old dissembler who lived out his lie
Lies here as if he did not fear to die.

2. *The Scarecrow*

His speech is spare,
An orchard scare
With battered hat:
Face rude and flat,
Whose painted eye
Jove's flashing doom
From broken sky
Can scarce illume:
The Thunderer
May strike his ear—
And no reply.

3. *With a Detective Story*

Old friend, you'll know by this how scholars live:
The scholar is a mere conservative,
A man whose being is in what is not—
The proud tradition and the poisoned plot.
He is bewildered in the things that were,
He thrives on sherry and the murderer,
And with his bottle on a rainy night
By Aristotle's saws brings crimes to light.
    So with this murderer may you make merry,
    And we'll redeem him with a glass of sherry.

4.

Jove courted Danäe with golden love,
But you're not Danäe, and I'm not Jove.

5. *The Lover's Ghost Returns to the Underworld*

Farewell, false love! Dawn and Lethean doom
Recall me. Where I go you too must come.
Others possess you here: there, mine alone,
You shall sleep with me, grinding bone to bone.

6.

Homer was poor. His scholars live at ease
Making as many Homers as you please,
And every Homer furnishes a book.
Though guests be parasitic on the cook
The moral is: *It is the guest who dines.*
I'll write a book to prove I wrote these lines.

7.

Time heals not: it extends a sorrow's scope
As goldsmiths gold, which we may wear like hope.

AUGUST HAIL

In late summer the wild geese
In the white draws are flying.
The grain beards in the blue peace.
The weeds are drying.

The hushed sky breeds hail.
Who shall revenge unreason?
Wheat headless in the white flail
Denies the season.

MONTANA PASTORAL

I am no shepherd of a child's surmises.
I have seen fear where the coiled serpent rises,

Thirst where the grasses burn in early May
And thistle, mustard, and the wild oat stay.

There is dust in this air. I saw in the heat
Grasshoppers busy in the threshing wheat.

So to this hour. Through the warm dusk I drove
To blizzards sifting on the hissing stove,

And found no images of pastoral will,
But fear, thirst, hunger, and this huddled chill.

There is no stillness in this wood.
The quiet of this clearing
Is the denial of my hearing
The sounds I should.

There is no vision in this glade.
This tower of sun revealing
The timbered scaffoldage is stealing
Essence from shade.

Only my love is love's ideal.
The love I could discover
In these recesses knows no lover,
Is the unreal,

The undefined, unanalysed,
Unabsolute many;
It is antithesis of any,
In none comprised.

AUTUMN

Gather the heart! The leaves
Fall in the red day. Grieves
No man more than the season.
Indifference is my guide.

Heart mellow and hope whirling
In a wild autumn hurling
Is time, and not time's treason.
And fatigue is my bride.

But say what moralist
Shall in himself subsist?
The tried. And you, occasion,
Far in my heart shall hide.

I have watched trains recede
Into that distance. Heed,
O heed not their persuasion
Who in no lands abide!

This pool in a pure frame,
This mirror of the vision of my nàme,
   Is a fiction
On the unrippled surface of reflection.

I see a willowed pool
Where the flies skim. Its angles have no rule.
   In no facet
Is the full vision imaged or implicit.

I've heard, in such a place
Narcissus sought the vision of his face.
   If the water
Concealed it, could he, drowning, see it better?

I know both what I see
And what I think, to alter and to be,
   And the vision
Of this informs that vision of confusion.

> In anima hominis dominatur violentia
> rationis.
> > —St. Bonaventure.

> Qui ne sait que la vue de chats, de rats,
> l'écrasement d'un charbon, etc., emportent
> la raison hors des gonds?
> > —Pascal.

Yes, we are all
By sense or thought
　　Distraught.
The violence of reason rules
　　The subtle Schools;
A falling ember has unhinged Pascal.

I know such men
Of wild perceptions.
　　Conceptions
Cold as the serpent and as wise
　　Have held my eyes:
Their fierce impersonal forms have moved my pen.

BOOKPLATE

Read me, ere age
Blot out this line.
Then will thy page,
Secure and whole
Though flaked like mine,
Pray for my soul,
And mine for thine.

The Judge Is Fury

1947

These the assizes: here the charge, denial,
Proof and disproof: the poem is the trial.
Experience is defendant, and the jury
Peers of tradition, and the judge is fury.

THE PHOENIX

More than the ash stays you from nothingness!
Nor here nor there is a consuming pyre!
Your essence is in infinite regress
That burns with varying consistent fire,
Mythical bird that bears in burying!

I have not found you in exhausted breath
That carves its image on the Northern air,
I have not found you on the glass of death
Though I am told that I shall find you there,
Imperturbable in the final cold,

There where the North wind shapes white cenotaphs,
There where snowdrifts cover the fathers' mound,
Unmarked but for these wintry epitaphs,
Still are you singing there without sound,
Your mute voice on the crystal embers flinging.

EXPERIENCE

When I was young I said,
"Affection is secure.
It is not forced or led."
No longer sure

Of the least certainty
I have erased my mind
As mendicants who see
Mimic the blind.

NOON

I have heard the self's stir,
Anonymous
And low, as on the stair
At time of Angelus

The worshippers repeat
An exorcism—
The angled clock's repute
Conjured with chrism.

Closed in a final rain
Clouds are complete,
Vows of shadowful light
Are vain,
And every hour is late.

Pride is a sky ingrown,
Selfishly fond,
By the edged sun nor found
Nor known,
But in the dusk defined.

RIPENESS IS ALL

Let us not live with Lear—
Not ever at extremes
Of ecstasy and fear,
Joy in what only seems,
Rage in the madman's hut
Or on the thunderous hill,
Crying *To kill, to kill!*
Nor in a blind desire
To sire we know not what
Ravish the eternal Will.

The rabbit crossed and dodged and turned—
I'd swear she neither saw nor heard
But ran for pleasure, unconcerned,
Erratic as a garden bird,

Timid and shy, but not afraid.
Say that her life was in the chase,
Yet it was nothing that God made
But wild blood glorying in a race

Through the cornfields of the lower Kaw.
My horse was tired before she fell.
Love does not work by natural law,
But as it is it's just as well,

For when the dogs retreated, fought,
And circled the embarrassed doe,
The doe moved only to be caught,
Quite pleased to be encircled so,

And I sat still, gun at my side.
Esteem and wonder stayed desire.
The kill is down. Time will abide.
Time to remember and inquire.

COFFEE

When I awoke with cold
And looked for you, my dear,
And the dusk inward rolled,
Not light or dark, but drear,

Unabsolute, unshaped,
That no glass can oppose,
I fled not to escape
Myself, but to transpose.

I have so often fled
Wherever I could drink
Dark coffee and there read
More than a man would think

That I say I waste time
For contemplation's sake:
In an uncumbered clime
Minute inductions wake,

Insight flows in my pen.
I know nor fear nor haste.
Time is my own again.
I waste it for the waste.

TO A FRIEND, ON HER EXAMINATION FOR
THE DOCTORATE IN ENGLISH

After these years of lectures heard,
Of papers read, of hopes deferred,
Of days spent in the dark stacks
In learning the impervious facts
So well you can dispense with 'em,
Now that the final day has come
When you shall answer name and date
Where fool and scholar judge your fate
What have you gained?
                A learnèd grace
And lines of knowledge on the face,
A spirit weary but composed
By true perceptions well-disposed,
A soft voice and historic phrase
Sounding the speech of Tudor days,
What ignorance cannot assail
Or daily novelty amaze,
Knowledge enforced by firm detail.

What revels will these trials entail!
What gentle wine confuse your head
While gossip lingers on the dead
Till all the questions wash away,
For you have learned, not what to say,
But how the saying must be said.

PASSION

Passion is never fact
And never in a kiss,
For it is pure unact,
All other than the this.

It is love's negative,
Love's furious potency,
Distinct from which we live
In the affirmed to be.

And as love's passive form
Is not this form I see
But all the loves that swarm
In the unwilled to be,

So in this actual kiss,
Unfaithful, I am true:
I realize in this
All passion, act, and you.

You are the problem I propose,
My dear, the text my musings glose:
I call you for convenience love.
By definition you're a cause
Inferred by necessary laws—
You are so to the saints above.
But in this shadowy lower life
I sleep with a terrestrial wife
And earthy children I beget.
Love is a fiction I must use,
A privilege I can abuse,
And sometimes something I forget.

Now, in the heavenly other place
Love is in the eternal mind
The luminous form whose shade she is,
A ghost discarnate, thought defined.
She was so to my early bliss,
She is so while I comprehend
The forms my senses apprehend,
And in the end she will be so.

Her whom my hands embrace I kiss,
Her whom my mind infers I know.
The one exists in time and space
And as she was she will not be;
The other is in her own grace
And is *She is* eternally.

Plato! you shall not plague my life.
I married a terrestrial wife.
And Hume! she is not mere sensation
In sequence of observed relation.
She has two forms—ah, thank you, Duns!—,
I know her in both ways at once.
I knew her, yes, before I knew her,
And by both means I must construe her,
And none among you shall undo her.

ENVOI

Hear me, whom I betrayed
While in this spell I stayed,
Anger, cathartic aid,
Hear and approve my song!

See from this sheltered cove
The symbol of my spell
Calm for adventure move,
Wild in repose of love,
Sea-going on a shell
In a moist dream. How long—
Time to which years are vain—
I on this coastal plain,
Rain and rank weed, raw air,
Served that fey despair,
Far from the lands I knew!

Winds of my country blew
Not with such motion—keen,
Stinging, and I as lean,
Savage, direct, and bitten,
Not pitying and unclean.

Anger, my ode is written.

FORGIVENESS

What is it to forgive?
It is not to forget,
To forfeit memory
　　In which I live.
It is to be in debt
To those who injure me.

If then I shall forgive
And consciously resign
My claim in love's estate
　　In which I live,
Know that the choice is mine
And is the same as hate.

Say then that I forgive.
I choose indignity
In which my passions burn
　　While I shall live—
O not for Charity!
But for my old concern.

APOLOGY

Simplicity assuages
With grace the damaged heart—
So would I in these pages
If will were art.

But the best engineer
Of metre, rhyme, and thought
Can only tool each gear
To what he sought

If chance with craft combines
In the predestined space
To lend his damaged lines
Redeeming grace.

ON A NICE BOOK

Your book affords
The peace of art,
Within whose boards
The passive heart

Impassive sleeps,
And like pressed flowers,
Though scentless, keeps
The scented hours.

ARS AMORIS

Speak to her heart!
That manic force
When wits depart
Forbids remorse.

Dream with her dreaming
Until her lust
Seems to her seeming
An act of trust!

Do without doing!
Love's wilful potion
Veils the ensuing,
And brief, commotion.

Evil is any this or this
Pursued beyond hypothesis.

It is the scribbling of affection
On the blank pages of perfection.

Evil is presentness bereaved
Of all the futures it conceived,

Wilful and realized restriction
Of the insatiate forms of fiction.

It is this poem, or this act.
It is this absolute of fact.

CONVALESCENCE

I found that consciousness itself betrays
Silence, the fever of my harried days.

In the last circle of infirmity
Where I almost attained simplicity—

So to recite as if it were not said,
So to renounce as if one lost instead—

My unabandoned soul withdrew abhorred.
I knew oblivion was its own reward,

But pride is life, and I had longed for death
Only in consciousness of indrawn breath.

TO MY DAIMON

Self-knower, self-aware,
Accomplice in despair!

Silence and shade increase
In corridors of peace

Till in a chapeled prayer
Warm grace wells from despair—

But if my heart offend me,
Daimon, can you defend me?

Who know myself within
The sinner and the sin.

The music of your feeling has its form,
And its symphonic solitude affirms
The resonance of self, remote and warm,
With private acmes at appointed terms.

So yours, so mine. And no one overhears.
O sealed composer of an endless past,
Rejoice that in that harmony of spheres
Pythagoras and Protagoras fuse at last!

THE SOLIPSIST

There is no moral treason—
Others are you. Your *hence*
Is personal consequence,
Desire is reason.

There is no moral strife—
None falls in the abysm
Who dwells there, solipsism
His way of life.

I have been here. Dispersed in meditation,
I sense the traces of the old surmise—
Passion dense as fatigue, faithful as pain,
As joy foreboding. O my void, my being
In the suspended sources of experience,
Massive in promise, unhistorical
Being of unbeing, of all futures full,
Unrealised in none, how love betrays you,
Turns you to process and a fluid fact
Whose future specifies its past, whose past
Precedes it, and whose history is its being.

DISTRACTION

I have distracted time.
In a full day your face
Has only its own place.
Tired from irrelevance
I sleep, and dream by chance,
Till passion can exact
No faith, and fails in act,
Till timelessness recedes
Beneath the apparent needs
Of a distracted time.

Plato, despair!
We prove by norms
How numbers bear
Empiric forms,

How random wrong
Will average right
If time be long
And error slight,

But in our hearts
Hyperbole
Curves and departs
To infinity.

Error is boundless.
Nor hope nor doubt,
Though both be groundless,
Will average out.

MEDITATION ON A MEMOIR

Who knows his will?
Who knows what mood
His hours fulfil?
His griefs conclude?

Surf of illusion
Spins from the deep
And skilled delusion
Sustains his sleep.

When silence hears
In its delight
The tide of tears
In the salt night,

And stirs, and tenses,
Who knows what themes,
What lunar senses,
Compel his dreams?

TO THE READER

Time will assuage.
Time's verses bury
Margin and page
In commentary,

For gloss demands
A gloss annexed
Till busy hands
Blot out the text,

And all's coherent.
Search in this gloss
No text inherent:
The text was loss.

The gain is gloss.

EPIGRAMS: A JOURNAL

1.

Each that I loved is now my enemy
To whom I severally inscribe this journal,
Who was defrauded of my vanity,
Peeled like a grain of wheat to the white kernel.

2.

I know not what I am. I think I know
Much of the circumstance in which I flow.
But knowledge is not power; I am that flow
Of history and of percept which I know.

3.

If I can't know myself it's something gained
To help my enemy to know his sin—
Especially since in him it's only feigned,
For the ideal exemplar lies within.

4.

Give not yourself to apology.
Yourself know, and slyly surprise
Passion, rework it, and let be.
Who is as he is is most wise.

5. *With a book of clavier music*

Discursive sense, unthought, unclear,
Is in this music planned:
Error is not of nature here
But of the human hand.

6.

My dear, though I have left no sigh
Carved on your stone, yet I still cherish
Your name and your flesh will not die
Till I and my descendants perish.

7.

All hastens to its end. If life and love
Seem slow it is their ends we're ignorant of.

8.

If wisdom, as it seems it is,
Be the recovery of some bliss
From the conditions of disaster—
Terror the servant, man the master—
It does not follow we should seek
Crises to prove ourselves unweak.
Much of our lives, God knows, is error,
But who will trifle with unrest?
These fools who would solicit terror,
Obsessed with being unobsessed,
Professionals of experience
Who have disasters to withstand them
As if fear never had unmanned them,
Flaunt a presumptuous innocence.

I have preferred indifference.

9.

Within this mindless vault
Lie *Tristan* and *Isolt*
Tranced in each other's beauties.
They had no other duties.

10.

Grief restrains grief as dams torrential rain,
And time grows fertile with extended pain.

11.

When I shall be without regret
And shall mortality forget,
When I shall die who lived for this,
I shall not miss the things I miss.
And you who notice where I lie
Ask not my name. It is not I.

12.

I was concerned for you and keep that part
In these days, irrespective of the heart:
And not for friendship, not for love, but cast
In that role by the presence of the past.

13. *On the cover of my first book*

This garish and red cover made me start.
I who amused myself with quietness
Am here discovered. In this flowery dress
I read the wild wallpaper of my heart.

14.

What is this visage? in what fears arrayed?
This ghost I conjured though that ghost was laid?
The vision of a vision still unstayed
By my voice, still by its own fears dismayed!

15.

Deep summer, and time pauses. Sorrow wastes
To a new sorrow. While time heals time hastes.

16.

The dry soul rages. The unfeeling feel
With the dry vehemence of the unreal.
So I in the Idea of your arms, unwon,
Am as the real in the unreal undone.

17.

Dear, if unsocial privacies obsess me,
If to my exaltations I be true,
If memories and images possess me,
Yes, if I love you, what is that to you?
My folly is no passion for collusion.
I cherish my illusions as illusion.

18.

Deep sowing of our shame, rage of our need,
Gross shadow of Idea, impersonal seed,
Unclothed desire! the malice of your thrust
Is his to use who takes his love on trust.

19.

In this child's game where you grow warm and warmer,
And new grand passions still exceed the former,
In what orgasm of high sentiment
Will you conclude and sleep at last content?

20.

After some years *Bohemian* came to this—
This Maenad with hair down and gaping kiss
Wild on the barren edge of under fifty.
She would finance his art if he were thrifty.

21.

Genius is born and made: this heel who mastered
By infinite pains his trade was born a bastard.

22.

I showed some devils of a moral kind
To a good friend who had a Freudian mind.
Doctor, there was no need for therapy.
I should have had myself to comfort me.

23.

Dark thoughts are my companions. I have wined
With lewdness and with crudeness, and I find
Love is my enemy, dispassionate hate
Is my redemption though it come too late—
Though I come to it with a broken head
In the cat-house of the dishevelled dead.

24.

Action is memoir: you may read my story
Even in pure thought—scandal in allegory.

25. *Motto for a sun dial*

I who by day am function of the light
Am constant and invariant by night.

26. *History of ideas*

God is love. Then by conversion
Love is God, and sex conversion.

27. *On the Calculus*

From almost naught to almost all I flee,
And *almost* has almost confounded me,
Zero my limit, and infinity.

28.

Soft found a way to damn me undefended:
I was forgiven who had not offended.

29.

Kiss me goodbye, to whom I've only been
Cause for uncloistered virtue, not for sin.

30.

This *Humanist* whom no beliefs constrained
Grew so broad-minded he was scatter-brained.

31.

He weeps and sleeps with Dido, calls him cad
Who followed God, and finds real Didos bad.

32.

This is my curse. *Pompous,* I pray
That you believe the things you say
And that you live them, day by day.

33.

Silence is noisome, but the loud logician
Raises more problems by their definition.
Hence let your discourse be a murmured charm
And so ambiguous none hears its harm.

34.

How we desire desire! Joy of surcease
In joy's fulfillment is bewildered peace,
And harsh renewal. Life in fear of death
Will trivialize the void with hurrying breath,
With harsh indrawal. Nor love nor lust impels us.
Time's hunger to be realised compels us.

35.

Hang up your weaponed wit
Who were destroyed by it.
If silence fails, then grace
Your speech with commonplace
And studiously amaze
Your audience with his phrase.
He will commend your wit
When you abandon it.

36.

The self is terrified, shade calls to shade,
Ghost destroys ghost whose ghost springs undismayed,
And fear regresses to infinity.
I know the spell in the mythology
Of this despair, I know love's charms affright
Psychotic goblins in the Gothic night,
I know your arms. Dear, in that incantation
Despair in joy attains its consummation.

37.

The scholar of theology and science
Who falls in love must in good faith affiance
Love and his trades; must prove the commonplace
Of his divine research, *Love goes by grace,*
Never by merit; judge by divination
Supernal from infernal visitation;
And risk his faith. As scientist he tries
By the inductive leap, immense surmise,
To force the future to confirm his guess —
Though predisposed toward ill or good success,
Pledged to the issue. So he may discover
As scholar truth, sincerity as lover.

38.

Dear, my familiar hand in love's own gesture
Gives irresponsive absence flesh and vesture.

39.
Death in this music dwells. I cease to be
In this attentive, taut passivity.

40. *To a Student*

Fiction, but memoir. Here you know
Motive and act who made them so.
Life falls in scenes; its tragedies
Close in contrived catastrophes.
Much is evasion. Some years pass
With *Some years later.* In this glass
Reflection sees reflection's smile
And self-engrossment is good style.

Fiction is fiction: its one theme
Is your allegiance to your scheme.
Memoir is memoir: there your heart
Awaits the judgment of your art.
But memoir in fictitious guise
Is telling truth by telling lies.

41. *A is A: Monism refuted*

The Monist who reduced the swarm
Of being to a single form,
Emptying the universe for fun,
Required two A's to think them one.

42. *With a copy of Swift's Works*

Underneath this pretty cover
Lies Vanessa's, Stella's lover.
You that undertake this story
For his life nor death be sorry
Who the Absolute so loved
Motion to its zero moved,
Till immobile in that chill
Fury hardened in the will,
And the trivial, bestial flesh
In its jacket ceased to thresh,
And the soul none dare forgive
Quiet lay, and ceased to live.

43.

In whose will is our peace? Thou happiness,
Thou ghostly promise, to thee I confess
Neither in thine nor love's nor in that form
Disquiet hints at have I yet been warm;
And if I rest not till I rest in thee
Cold as thy grace, whose hand shall comfort me?

Doctor Drink

1950

1.

In the thirtieth year of life
I took my heart to be my wife,

And as I turn in bed by night
I have my heart for my delight.

No other heart may mine estrange
For my heart changes as I change,

And it is bound, and I am free,
And with my death it dies with me.

2. *Interview with Doctor Drink*

I have a fifth of therapy
In the house, and transference there.
Doctor, there's not much wrong with me,
Only a sick rattlesnake somewhere

In the house, if it be there at all,
But the lithe mouth is coiled. The shapes
Of door and window move. I call.
What is it that pulls down the drapes,

Disheveled and exposed? Your rye
Twists in my throat: intimacy
Is like hard liquor. Who but I
Coil there and squat, and pay your fee?

3.

Lip was a man who used his head.
He used it when he went to bed
With his friend's wife, and with his friend,
With either sex at either end.

4. *Epitaph for Someone or Other*

Naked I came, naked I leave the scene,
And naked was my pastime in between.

5.

All in due time: love will emerge from hate,
And the due deference of truth from lies.
If not quite all things come to those who wait
They will not need them: in due time one dies.

6.

Dear child whom I begot,
Forgive me if my page
Hymns not your helpless age,
For you are mine, and not:
Mine as sower and sown,
But in yourself your own.

7.

Life flows to death as rivers to the sea,
And life is fresh and death is salt to me.

8.

On a cold night I came through the cold rain
And false snow to the wind shrill on your pane
With no hope and no anger and no fear:
Who are you? and with whom do you sleep here

Trivial, Vulgar, and Exalted

Uncollected Poems and Epigrams

1959

1. *On* Doctor Drink

A reader (did he buy it, borrow, beg,
Or read it in a bookstore on one leg?)
Dislikes my book; calls it, to my discredit,
A book you can't put down before you've read it;
Yet in this paucity, this drouth of phrases,
There are as many as in children phases:
The trivial, vulgar, and exalted jostle
Each other in a way to make the apostle
Of culture and right feeling shudder faintly.
It is a shudder that affects the saintly.
It is a shudder by which I am faulted.
I like the trivial, vulgar, and exalted.

2.

Here lies my wife. Eternal peace
Be to us both with her decease.

3.

My name is Ebenezer Brown.
I carted all the trash of town
For sixty years. On the last day
I trust my Lord will cart me away.

4.

I married in my youth a wife.
She was my own, my very first.
She gave the best years of her life.
I hope nobody gets the worst.

5.

Here lies New Critic who would fox us
With his poetic paradoxes.
Though he lies here rigid and quiet,
If he could speak he would deny it.

6.

You wonder why *Drab* sells her love for gold?
To have the means to buy it when she's old.

7.

You ask me how *Contempt* who claims to sleep
With every woman that has ever been
Can still maintain that women are skin deep?
They never let him any deeper in.

8.

With every wife he can, and you know why?
Bold goes to bed because really he's shy.
And why I publish it none knows but I:
I publish it because really I'm shy.

9.

Bride loved old words, and found her pleasure marred
On the first night, her expectations jarred,
And thirty inches short of being a yard.

10.

Career was feminine, resourceful, clever.
You'd never guess to see her she felt ever
By a male world oppressed. How much they weigh!
Even her hand disturbed her as she lay.

11.

Your affair, my dear, need not be a mess.
See at the next table with what finesse,
With what witty tensions and what tense wit,
As intricate as courtship, the love-fated
Sir Gawain and the Fay at lunch commit
Faithful adultery unconsummated.

12.

The Elders at their services begin
With paper offerings. They release from sin
The catechumens on the couches lying
In visions, testimonies, prophesying:
Not, "Are you saved?" they ask, but in informal
Insistent query, "Brother, are you normal?"

13.

Arms and the man I sing, and sing for joy,
Who was last year all elbows and a boy.

14.

The man who goes for Christian resignation
Will find his attitude his occupation.

15.

Another novel, and the prostitute
And the initiate—I who have never known
The rite of artistry, or how to do it,
With meager manuscript sit here alone.

16.

And now you're ready who while she was here
Hung like a flag in a calm. Friend, though you stand
Erect and eager, in your eye a tear,
I will not pity you, or lend a hand.

17. *For a College Yearbook*

Somewhere on these bare rocks in some bare hall,
Perhaps unrecognized, wisdom and learning
Flash like a beacon on a sleeper's wall,
Ever distant and dark, ever returning.

18.

Love, receive Lais' glass, the famous whore,
In whose reflection you appear no more.

19.

I had gone broke, and got set to come back,
And lost, on a hot day and a fast track,
On a long shot at long odds, a black mare
By Hatred out of Envy by Despair.

20.

Friend, on this scaffold Thomas More lies dead
Who would not cut the Body from the Head.

21.

And what is love? Misunderstanding, pain,
Delusion, or retreat? It is in truth
Like an old brandy after a long rain,
Distinguished, and familiar, and aloof.

22. *Night-piece*

Three matches in a folder, you and me.
I sit and smoke, and now there's only two,
And one, and none: a small finality
In a continuing world, a thing to do.
And you, fast at your book, whose fingers keep
Its single place as you sift down to sleep.

23. *New York: 5 March 1957*

Lady, of anonymous flesh and face
In the half-light, in the rising embrace
Of my losses, in the dark dress and booth,
The stripper of the gawking of my youth,
Lady, I see not, care not, what you are.
I sit with beer and bourbon at this bar.

24.

Good Fortune, when I hailed her recently,
Passed by me with the intimacy of shame
As one that in the dark had handled me
And could no longer recollect my name.

25.

Love, at what distance mine!
On whose disdain I dine
Unfed, unfamished, I
In your hid counsels lie.
I know your lover, fear.
His presence is austere
As winter air. He trembles
Though the taut face dissembles.
I know him: I am he.

26. *The Aged Lover Discourses in the Flat Style*

There are, perhaps, whom passion gives a grace,
Who fuse and part as dancers on the stage,
But that is not for me, not at my age,
Not with my bony shoulders and fat face.
Yet in my clumsiness I found a place
And use for passion: with it I ignore
My gaucheries and yours, and feel no more
The awkwardness of the absurd embrace.

It is a pact men make, and seal in flesh,
To be so busy with their own desires
Their loves may be as busy with their own,
And not in union. Though the two enmesh
Like gears in motion, each with each conspires
To be at once together and alone.

27. *Horoscope*

Out of one's birth
The magi chart his worth;
They mark the influence
Of hour and day, and weigh what thence

Will come to be.
I in their cold sky see
Neither Venus nor Mars;
It is the past that cast the stars

That guide me now.
In winter when the bough
Has lost its leaves, the storm
That piled them deep will keep them warm.

Translations from the Latin

DECIMUS LABERIUS

An Old Actor Addresses Julius Caesar

Necessity, the impact of whose sidelong course
Many attempt to escape and only few succeed,
Whither have you thrust down, almost to his wits' ends,
Him whom flattery, whom never bribery
Could in his youth avail to shake him from his stand?
But see how easily an old man slips, and shows—
Moved by the complacency of this most excellent man—
Calm and complaisant, a submissive, fawning speech!
Yet naught to a conqueror could the gods themselves deny,
And who then would permit one man to say him nay?
I who existed sixty long years without stain,
A Roman Knight who went from his paternal gods,
Now return home a mime. And certainly today
I've lived out one more day than I should have lived.
Fortune, unrestrained in prosperity and ill,
Were it your pleasure with the lure and praise of letters
To shatter the very summit of my good name,
Why when I prospered, when my limbs were green with youth,
When I could satisfy an audience and such a man,
Did you not bend my suppleness and spit on me?
Now you cast me? Whither? What brought I to the stage?
The ornament of beauty, dignity of flesh,
Fire of the spirit, the music of a pleasing voice?
As twining ivy kills the stout heart of the tree,
So has senility in time's embrace destroyed me
And like a sepulchre I keep only a name.

Odes 1.9

See how resplendent in deep snow
Soracte stands, how straining trees
    Scarce can sustain their burden
        Now that the rivers congeal and freeze.

Thaw out the chill, still heaping more
Wood on the hearth: ungrudgingly
    Pour forth from Sabine flagons,
        O Thaliarchus, the ripened wine:

Leave all else to the gods. They soon
Will level on the yeasty deep
    Th' embattled tempests, stirring
        Cypress no more, nor agéd ash.

Tomorrow may no man divine.
This day that Fortune gives set down
    As profit, nor while young still
        Scorn the rewards of sweet dancing love,

So long as from your flowering days
Crabbed age delays. Now through the parks
    Soft whisperings toward nightfall
        Visit again at the trysting hour;

Now from her bower comes the charmed laugh,
Betrayer of the hiding girl;
    Now from her arm the forfeit
        Plundered, her fingers resisting not.

MARTIAL

Epigrams 1.33

In private she mourns not the late-lamented;
If someone's by her tears leap forth on call.
Sorrow, my dear, is not so easily rented.
They are true tears that without witness fall.

Epigrams 2.5

Believe me, sir, I'd like to spend whole days,
Yes, and whole evenings in your company,
But the two miles between your house and mine
Are four miles when I go there to come back.
You're seldom home, and when you are deny it,
Engrossed with business or with yourself.
Now, I don't mind the two mile trip to see you;
What I do mind is going four to not to.

MARTIAL

Epigrams 2.68

That I now call you by your name
Who used to call you sir and master,
You needn't think it impudence.
I bought myself with all I had.
He ought to sir a sir and master
Who's not himself, and wants to have
Whatever sirs and masters want.
Who can get by without a slave
Can get by, too, without a master.

Epigrams 4.69

You serve the best wines always, my dear sir,
And yet they say your wines are not so good.
They say you are four times a widower.
They say . . . A drink? I don't believe I would.

Silaae 5.4

What was my crime, youthful most gentle god,
What folly was it that I alone should lack,
Sweet Sleep, thy gifts? All herds, birds, beasts are still,
The curved mountains seem wearily asleep,
Streams rage with muted noise, the sea-wave falls,
And the still-nodding deep rests on the shore.
Seven times now returning Phoebe sees
My sick eyes stare, and so the morning star
And evening, so Tithonia glides by
My tears, sprinkling sad dew from her cool whip.
How, then, may I endure? Not though were mine
The thousand eyes wherewith good Argus kept
But shifting watch, nor all his flesh awake.
But now, alas! If this long night some lover
In his girl's arms should willingly repel thee,
Thence come sweet Sleep! Nor with all thy power
Pour through my eyes—so may they ask, the many,
More happy—; touch me with thy wand's last tip,
Enough, or lightly pass with hovering step.

ST. AMBROSE

Aeterne Rerum Conditor

Builder eternally of things,
Thou rulest over night and day,
Disposing time in separate times
That Thou mayst lessen weariness;

Now crows the herald of the day,
Watchful throughout the wasting dark,
To walkers in the night a clock
Marking the hours of dark and dawn.

The morning star arises now
To free the obscure firmament;
Now every gang and prowling doom
Forsakes the dark highways of harm.

The sailor now regathers strength,
The channels of the sea grow calm;
And now Peter, the living rock,
Washes his guilt in the last crow.

Then quickly let us rise and go;
The cock stirs up the sleepy-head,
And chides again the lie-a-bed;
The cock convicts them who deny.

And to cock-crow our hopes reply;
Thy grace refills our ailing hearts;
The sword of brigandage is hid;
And faith returns where faith had fled.

Jesu, look back on us who fall,
Straighten the conduct of our life;
If Thou lookst back, denials fail,
And guilt is melted in a tear.

Thou Light, illumine with Thy light
Our sleeping lethargy of soul;
Thy name the first our lips shall choose,
Discharging thus our vows to Thee.

The Confession of Bishop Golias

Inwardly fired with vehement wrath,
In bitterness I will speak my mind:
Made of material light as lath,
I am like a leaf tossed by the wind.

Though it were just for the wise and brave
To place their seat on the rock of will,
Fool, I am like the flowing wave
That under one sky is ever unstill.

I am borne on as a pilotless ship,
As a vagrant bird through the cloudy haze;
Ungoverned by reins, ungoverned by whip,
I gad with my kind, I follow their ways.

I walk the broad path in the fashion of youth,
Forgetful of virtue, entangled with sin;
Avid of pleasure more than of truth
I die in soul but take care of my skin.

Most worthy prelate, your pardon I pray,
I die a good death, swing on a sweet rope,
At sight of the ladies I still get gay;
Whom I cannot by touch, I sin with in hope.

Who placed on a pyre will not burn in the fire?
Or dallying at Pavia can keep himself chaste?
Where Venus goes hunting young men for hire,
Drooping her eyelids and fixing her face.

Hippolytus placed in Pavia today
Would not be Hippolytus "when the dawn came";
To the bedroom of Venus still runs the broad way,
Nor in all those towers is the tower of shame.

Again, I'm charged with playing strip poker:
When play casts me out in my naked skin,
Shivering, I sweat while my mind plays stoker,
And I write better verse than I did within.

The tavern, thirdly, I note in this summing
Up of the life I will ever have led
Till I hear the holy angels coming,
Singing rest eternal unto the dead.

For I propose in the tavern to die
That wine may be near when the throat grows hard,
And the chorus of angels may joyfully cry,
"O Lord, be kindly to this drunkard."

The lamp of the soul is lighted by wine,
Sotted with nectar it flies to the sky;
Wine of the tavern is far more divine
Than watery wine that the priest raises high.

They say a poet should flee public places
And choose his seat in a quiet retreat:
He sweats, presses on, stays awake, and erases,
Yet comes back with scarcely one clear conceit.

The chorus of poets should fast and abstain,
Avoid public quarrels and brawls with their neighbors:
That they may compose what will ever remain,
They die in a cell, overcome by their labors.

Nature to such gives a suitable crown:
I never could write on an empty purse;
Myself when fasting a boy could knock down;
Thirsting and hunger I hate like a hearse.

Never's the spirit of poetry given
Except when the belly is fat and sleek;
While Bacchus is lord of my cerebral heaven,
Apollo moves through me and marvels I speak.

Behold, of my vice I was that informer
By whom your henchmen indicted me;
No one of them is his own accuser,
Though he hopes to sport through eternity.

So I stand before the blessed prelate
Urging that precept of our Lord wherein
He casts the first stone, nor spares the poet,
Whose heart is wholly devoid of sin.

I've charged myself with whatever I knew
And vomited up my long cherished dole;
The old life passes, gives way to the new;
Man notes appearance, Jove sees the soul.

Primate of Cologne, grant me your blessing,
Absolve the sinner who begs your grace;
Impose due penance on him confessing;
Whatever you bid I'll gladly embrace.

Rome

You that a stranger in mid-Rome seek Rome
And can find nothing in mid-Rome of Rome,
Behold this mass of walls, these abrupt rocks,
Where the vast theatre lies overwhelmed.
Here, here is Rome! Look how the very corpse
Of greatness still imperiously breathes threats!
The world she conquered, strove herself to conquer,
Conquered that nothing be unconquered by her.
Now conqueror Rome's interred in conquered Rome,
And the same Rome conquered and conqueror.
Still Tiber flows on swift waves to the sea.
Learn hence what Fortune can: the unmoved falls,
And the ever-moving will remain forever.